Charles Barkley

Additional titles in the Sports Reports *series:*

Michael Jordan
Star Guard
(0-89490-482-5)

Jim Kelly
Star Quarterback
(0-89490-446-9)

Chris Mullin
Star Forward
(0-89490-486-8)

Shaquille O'Neal
Star Center
(0-89490-656-9)

Cal Ripken, Jr.
Star Shortstop
(0-89490-485-X)

David Robinson
Star Center
(0-89490-483-3)

Barry Sanders
Star Running Back
(0-89490-484-1)

Deion Sanders
Star Athlete
(0-89490-652-6)

Emmitt Smith
Star Running Back
(0-89490-653-4)

Frank Thomas
Star First Baseman
(0-89490-659-3)

Thurman Thomas
Star Running Back
(0-89490-445-0)

Steve Young
Star Quarterback
(0-89490-654-2)

SPORTS REPORTS

Charles Barkley

Star Forward

Ron Knapp

ENSLOW PUBLISHERS, INC.
44 Fadem Road   P.O. Box 38
Box 699   Aldershot
Springfield, N.J. 07081   Hants GU12 6BP
U.S.A.   U.K.

Library of Congress Cataloging-in-Publication Data

Knapp, Ron.
    Charles Barkley : star forward / Ron Knapp.
       p. cm. — (Sports reports)
    Includes bibliographical references and index.
    Summary: A biography of the basketball superstar, from his childhood in Alabama through his years at Auburn University to his career with the Philadelphia 76ers and the Phoenix Suns.
    ISBN 0-89490-655-0
    1. Barkley, Charles, 1963- —Juvenile literature. 2. Basketball players—United States—Biography—Juvenile literature. [1. Barkley, Charles, 1963- . 2. Basketball players. 3. Afro-Americans—Biography.] I. Title. II. Series.
GV884.B28K53 1996
796.323'092—dc20
[B]
            95-38495
            CIP
            AC

Printed in the United States of America

10 9 8 7 6 5 4 3 2 1

Photo Credits: Auburn University, p. 37; Don Grayston, pp. 9, 28, 86, 89; Mitchell Layton Photography, pp. 11, 13, 33, 42, 46, 48, 51, 57, 59, 64, 69, 85; Norm Perdue, pp. 16, 19, 74, 76, 81.

Cover Illustration: Norm Perdue

Contents

1 Somebody Tough Enough 7

2 Jumping Over Fences 21

3 Getting Motivated 32

4 Rookie 40

5 A Troubled Team 50

6 Bad Luck 61

7 Olympic Hero and MVP 71

8 One More Goal 80

Chapter Notes 93

Career Statistics 100

Where to Write 101

Index 102

Chapter 1

Somebody Tough Enough

Charles Barkley almost did it all in 1993. For eight years, he had been with the Philadelphia 76ers, a team with a habit of trading away its best players. Every season he had great statistics, but the team wasn't good enough to make it to the NBA Finals.

The Phoenix Suns were frustrated, too. They usually had great seasons, but died in the playoffs. Better teams always beat them by pushing them around under the basket.

Back in 1992, Lionel Hollins, a Suns assistant coach, had said, "What we need is a Barkley type."[1] Phoenix needed somebody who was tough enough to push back. The rest of the coaching staff agreed they wanted somebody like Charles. What they got was the real thing.

Less than a month after the 1991–92 season ended, Phoenix traded three players (Jeff Hornacek, Tim Perry, and Andrew Lang) to Philadelphia for Barkley.

He knew why the Suns wanted him. "He'll do everything he can to win a championship . . . ," said Coach Paul Westphal. "The reason he's had the kind of career he's had is that he plays to win. And he's very good at it. And if you play to win, you want to win championships."[2]

By 1992 Charles had been playing on teams for sixteen years, and none of them, not junior high, high school, college, or pro, had ever won a championship. He planned to change that in Phoenix. With great teammates like Dan Majerle, Kevin Johnson, and Danny Ainge, he expected to make it to the NBA Finals.

In the fall of 1992 the Suns exploded, winning twenty-one of their first twenty-five games. Charles was red hot, getting 44 points in a 111–107 loss to the Los Angeles Clippers on November 21. A month later he grabbed 23 rebounds as the Los Angeles Lakers fell, 116–100. Then on January 27, he had 24 rebounds as Phoenix nipped the Minnesota Timberwolves in overtime, 117–116.

When the regular season ended, Barkley had 1,944 points for a 25.6-per-game average, the fifth

Charles Barkley had one of the best seasons of his career in 1992–93. Not only was he named the NBA's most valuable player, the Phoenix Suns ended the season with their best record ever.

best in the league. His rebounding totals (928 for 12.2) were sixth best. He led the league in technical fouls (32) and ejections (4). But the most important total of all was the Phoenix team record of 62–20, the best in the NBA. It was the most victories ever for a Suns team.

For his magnificent season, Barkley was named the league's Most Valuable Player. It was the first time in seven years that anybody besides Magic Johnson or Michael Jordan had been MVP. By then, Johnson had retired, but Charles beat Jordan as well as such greats as Hakeem Olajuwon, Patrick Ewing, and Shaquille O'Neal for the honor.

It had been a great regular season and Barkley was having the time of his life. In fact, in a late-season game against the Portland Trail Blazers, his enthusiasm almost wrecked the Suns' season. As time ran out, Charles hit the winning basket, then celebrated by jumping into Kevin Johnson's arms. Have you ever had a 250-pound athlete jump into your arms? It can be pretty dangerous. Johnson, who's only six feet one inch tall and 190 pounds, cringed in pain as soon as Barkley hit him.

The hug strained Johnson's knee and kept him from playing his best as the playoffs began. In the first round, the Suns dropped their first two games

FACT

Michael Jordan is one of the most successful superstars in the history of sports. In college, he sank the winning basket for North Carolina in the 1982 NCAA title game. In Chicago, he won the National Basketball Association MVP award three times and led the Bulls to three consecutive world championships.

Suns guard Kevin Johnson was a pivotal player in the team's great 1992–93 season.

at home to the Lakers, before winning the next three and advancing.

Phoenix and the San Antonio Spurs split their first four games. Then in Game 5, David Robinson and the Spurs were ahead by one point midway through the fourth quarter. That's when Charles went wild, scoring thirteen unanswered points. Two of the shots were three-pointers, with Robinson falling over him and picking up fouls. When he was done, San Antonio was finished. "I played probably the best game of my life. We were down the whole game and I scored twenty points in the fourth quarter, and it was just unbelieveable."[3] Phoenix won 109–97.

Game 6 was a fantastic back-and-forth battle between Barkley and Robinson. With eleven seconds left, Robinson dropped in two free throws to tie the game 100–100. The Suns charged down the court. With just under two seconds to go, Barkley went up with a shot from the top of the key. Robinson leaped to block it, but the ball was over him and through the hoop. Phoenix won 102–100.

"If you want to be great," Charles said, "you have to be willing to take the big shot—anywhere and anytime. I always expect to hit the big shot."[4]

Then came the Seattle SuperSonics. After six games, the teams were tied at three games apiece.

David Robinson battled it out with Barkley in the second round of the 1993 NBA playoffs.

The winner of the seventh match would advance to the NBA Finals. By then Charles was exhausted and hurting. He spent the day before the last game soaking in Epsom salts and trying to heal his tired body.

In the decisive Game 7, the Sonics had a 37–33 lead in the second quarter. The Suns seemed listless and angry. Instead of playing hard, they were whining about the mistakes their teammates were making. Charles got mad. "Shut up and play," he told them.[5] And they did.

Phoenix got eight straight points and led by six points at the half. The Suns opened the third quarter with a 14–2 run. Barkley scored eight of those points and assisted on four others. When it was over, he had 44 points and 24 rebounds. The Suns' 123–110 victory put them into the NBA Finals.

During the Seattle series, Barkley had tried to keep his teammates loose by joking about their opponents. Who would he rather face—Jordan's Chicago Bulls or Ewing's New York Knicks? "I hope the Bulls make it so [Michael] and I can play golf. See, Patrick doesn't play golf. I think New York will win, but me and Michael would have some good golf matches."[6]

Barkley was wrong. Chicago beat the Knicks 4 games to 2. Now the Suns would have to face the

Bulls, and Jordan wasn't thinking about golf. He and his teammates were trying to take their third straight league championship.

Charles was confident. After the season the Suns had, he expected them to take the Bulls.[?] "God wanted us to win the championship," he said on nationwide television. "I talked to him the other night."[7]

But Chicago jumped out to a 46–26 lead midway through the second quarter of the Finals opener. Phoenix managed to close the gap to 88–85 with 4:25 left, but then Jordan went to work. He scored 14 fourth-quarter points, and the Bulls won 100–92.

Barkley told the Suns fans not to worry. "Let's not go crazy after one game. Let's wait until Game 2. If we lose that, then we can go crazy."[8] Chicago jumped out to another big lead in the second game, but the Suns came back to tie it up early in the fourth quarter. Charles's layup with 10:36 to go gave Phoenix a 91–89 lead. The game seesawed back and forth as Barkley scored 42 points and totaled 13 rebounds. But Chicago wound up on top, 111–108.

The Suns were down two games to none. Despite heroic efforts they had lost the first two games at their home arena. On top of that, Charles had severely bruised his elbow when he fell in Game 2. In the locker room before the next game, it

Barkley put all he had into the Suns-Bulls NBA Finals.

hurt so badly he couldn't raise his right arm above his head. The team doctor jabbed a needle into the elbow to drain fluid and ease the swelling. Then a bandage was slapped on and Charles stepped onto the court. Playing with one good arm, he scored 24 points and grabbed 19 rebounds as Phoenix won in triple overtime, 129–121.

But after the Bulls came back with a 111–105 win, they were just a game away from the NBA championship. The champagne was ready for a locker-room celebration. Chicago city officials feared the celebration would spill out of the Chicago Stadium into the nearby streets. They were afraid the party would turn into a riot. Store owners began boarding up their windows.

The Suns were in desperate shape. Time for another Barkley joke. "We have to win this game and save the city!" he said.[9] If Phoenix won, there would be no celebration in Chicago, and no chance of a riot. His teammates laughed and loosened up once again. The Bulls thought they could already taste the champagne when they stepped onto the court, but Charles and the Suns blasted them 108–98.

The Bulls' lead in the series was now three to two. If the Suns could win the next two games in Phoenix, they would be the champions. "I believe it, 100 percent, that it's our destiny to win the championship," Barkley said.[10] This time he wasn't joking.

The Bulls grabbed an early lead in Game 6 and it looked like they were going to coast to the title. It wasn't until the fourth quarter that Phoenix fans really had something to cheer about. The Suns outscored the Bulls 9–1 to tie the game 88–88. With just 2:23 left, Phoenix was up, 98–94. It looked like the Bulls had run out of steam. The home crowd was going crazy. If the Suns could hang on for the win, they would be one victory away from the title.

Michael Jordan has been called the greatest basketball player of all time, and he was not about to let his team's chance for a third straight title slip away. He drove to the basket for a layup that made it 98–96.

The Suns had to hold off the Bulls for another minute. But as the seconds ticked away, Jordan passed to Scottie Pippen, who hit Horace Grant near the basket. Grant threw the ball out to John Paxson, who was standing just outside the three-point line. Paxson unleashed a beautiful shot with less than four seconds to go. It was good for 3 points! Chicago won the game, 99–98!

Jordan and his teammates had their third consecutive NBA championship. Barkley and the Suns

When the Suns met the Bulls in the 1993 NBA Finals, Barkley thought the time for his first championship had finally come. It was a crushing blow to him when the Suns lost in Game 6.

walked quietly off the court. Paxson's shot had ended the season and broken their hearts.

Now it hurt too much to joke, so Charles just told the truth. "We played as hard as we could. You can't do no more. I'm proud of my team."[11]

More than a year later, Barkley thought about how much the Finals loss had hurt. "Somewhere along the way I got lost. I let people convince me that I'm nothing if I don't win a championship. If I believe that, I'm stupid. But I believed it."[12]

Charles Barkley had been around long enough to know that he was something. He had done magnificent things on the basketball court, and he was one of the richest, most popular athletes in the world. Nothing could change that.

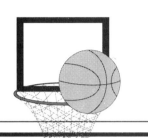

Chapter 2

Jumping Over Fences

Charles Wade Barkley was born on February 20, 1963, in Leeds, Alabama, a tiny town near Birmingham, the state's largest city.

When he was just a few days old, the doctors discovered he had anemia. His body didn't have enough red blood cells. To correct the problem, he would need a blood transfusion. Since Charles was so tiny, the doctors had a tough time finding a vein big enough for the needle. Finally they stuck it in his foot. He got his blood transfusion, and soon he was a healthy, happy baby.

"I was quite young when I had Charles . . .," said his mother, Charcey Glenn.[1] Frank Barkley, his dad, left town when his son was about a year old. Charcey took Charles to live with her mother, Johnnie Mae Edwards, and her husband, Adolphus. Since his own father wasn't around, Charles called Adolphus "Little Daddy." The older man got along well with the boy and continued to see him even after he and Johnnie Mae were divorced.

Charcey cleaned other people's homes for a living while Johnnie Mae worked as a beautician. "They made sure I had everything I needed," Charles said, "even though they had to go without paying bills."[2]

He has always figured that Leeds is a pretty good place to be from. Only about ten thousand people live there. It's a friendly town where people take care of each other. There aren't a lot of problems with gangs and crime. "In Leeds, one person dies a week and that's from old age," Charles said.[3] When he was growing up, there was a playground down the street from his home with a basketball court, and a vacant lot nearby for baseball.

Before he was born, schools in Leeds and throughout the South were segregated. White children went to one school, blacks to another. But when it was time for Charles to go to elementary school, laws were being passed that ended segregation. His mother now had a choice where to send him. She picked Leeds Elementary School, which had previously been reserved for the white children.

Charles was one of the first black students to attend, but he was treated well by most of his classmates there, and he liked the school. Years later, he said, "I enjoyed studying math," but Barkley was never much of a student.[4]

He was also not the most popular child in school. "He was a very shy kid," said his mother. "You know he was quiet."[5] Barkley's grandmother remembered the little boy's appearance: "He was on the chubby side and he was just as tall as he was chubby. The kids used to pick on him."[6] Some of the white boys at school gave him a rough time because of his race, and a few of his black neighbors teased him for going to the "white school." Charles stuck up for himself, and he had his share of fights, but usually he was a quiet, happy kid who didn't attract a lot of attention.

Charles's mother kept a close eye on him and helped steer him toward sports. "I played basketball mostly to keep out of trouble . . . ," he said. "It was the only fun Mama'd let me have."[7]

But his mother couldn't watch Charles every minute. When he was seven, he wanted to see if he could fly. He thought he was Superman. "So, cape and all, he jumped off the roof," said Mrs. Glenn. "The building was two stories high. Charles landed on his face, and knocked himself out."[8] The little

FACT

After the American Civil War, many schools in the South were segregated. That meant that black children couldn't attend the same schools as whites. Because of the efforts of Martin Luther King, Jr., and people like him, laws were written in the 1960s that made segregation illegal.

boy was bleeding, and he had a concussion, but he wasn't seriously hurt.

When Charles was nine, Frank Barkley finally came back to Leeds to visit his son. Then the boy went home with him to California for the summer. The visit didn't go well, and he rarely saw his dad again while he was growing up. ". . . I wish he had been there and hurt that he wasn't," Charles said years later. "I was very angry and very resentful. . . ."[9]

Meanwhile his mother had married Clee Glenn and had two more sons, Darryl and John. But when Charles was eleven, Mr. Glenn was killed in an automobile crash. Now Mrs. Glenn was left with three sons. Charles's grandmother was proud of the way Charles treated the new babies. "He was a father to his younger brothers because he grew up without a father."[10]

Barkley's mother was still busy trying to support her family, and Charles did what he could to help. "I would work two jobs and I would get up so early . . . I wouldn't have time to do anything, but by the time I got home from that second job at night, the house would be clean as a pin."[11] Charles wanted everything to be perfect for his mother. "He washed. He mopped. He would wax the linoleum floors. They were so shiny you could see yourself."[12]

FACT

Superman was one of the first comic book superheroes to appear in movies and on television. Because he was born on the planet Krypton under a red sun, Superman has superpowers. Bullets can't hurt him, and he can fly. He's been popular with kids since he first appeared in a 1938 comic book.

But while he was helping at home, Charles was also finding time to get into trouble. He began stealing snacks from stores near his home. One night a police car showed up when he and some friends took a few cakes. The car chased them for several blocks before the boys ran into the woods. Still the police followed. "They said 'freeze,'" Barkley said. Even though it was so dark they couldn't see, the boys kept running full speed through the woods. "The whole front of my leg was bleeding. I remember running into a tree going down. I'm scared stiff. . . ."[13]

But Charles got up and crawled as fast as he could. After going about fifty yards on his hands and knees, he was safe. The police never caught anybody that night. Some of his friends thought their escape was proof they could always outwit the police. They kept stealing; not Charles. He didn't want to risk being arrested and having to admit to his mother and grandmother that he was a thief. As he crawled away from the police that night, he decided, "This ain't the lifestyle I want."[14]

If he was going to stay out of trouble, Barkley figured he had to stay busy. To fill up his time, he decided to concentrate on basketball. Almost twenty years later when he was an NBA superstar, he was, of course, very glad he had decided to stick with sports. Without basketball, he was afraid he might have wound up in prison with some of his friends.

As a young teenager, Charles liked basketball, but he wasn't very good at it. His biggest problem was that he wasn't shaped like a basketball player. He wasn't tall enough, and he was still chubby. In his first year at Leeds Junior High School, he didn't even make the team. But he kept practicing—and he kept out of trouble.

At Leeds High School, he still wasn't very good, and he didn't make the ninth grade team. The coach, Billy Coupland, said the problem was his height. "It was just hard for him to compete. Plus his shot in high school wasn't that good."[15]

Charles wanted so badly to play that it hurt. Sometimes he was so upset he cried to his mother, "I am good enough to play on the varsity . . . if they'll only give me a chance."[16] But Charles did more than just cry. He went to work. He couldn't do anything about being short, but he could work on his speed, his jumping, and his shooting. He spent hours every day on the court down the street. Usually, he was by himself. He figured he should be shooting and rebounding, not playing games. So that's what he did over and over: shooting and rebounding.

A good athlete needs lots of endurance, so Charles tried to get in better shape by jumping rope for hours and running through the streets of Leeds.

To be a good rebounder, a basketball player needs to jump, so Charles began hopping over the three-and-a-half-foot chain-link fence around his yard. He didn't take a running start. He just stood next to the fence and jumped over it. Then he hopped back over from the other side. Over and over. His mother and grandmother sat on the porch and watched him. "He would run for hours in the hot sun," said Mrs. Glenn. "And he'd jump over that fence. I'd watch him fall down and hurt himself, and I would want him to stop. But he told me, 'Momma, I'm going to play in the NBA.' And he meant it. Nothing was going to stop him."[17]

Already Charles was planning on using basketball to help his family. "In high school, my number one priority in life is to make life easier on my mother and grandmother, so I'm thinking just go to college for free."[18] He knew if he was good enough at basketball he could get a scholarship to attend college.

Barkley had big goals and he was working hard to achieve them, but he knew he really didn't have much chance to get a scholarship, much less sign an NBA contract. His teammates thought he was crazy,

Despite his stocky build, Charles Barkley has great jumping ability—an important skill for an NBA player.

and they laughed at him. "I had no hope," he said later. "Most people who brag are insecure, and I was insecure because I wasn't that good. There were so many talented guys on my team in high school."[19] When he was in eleventh grade, Charles spent most of his time on the bench. He was still only five feet ten inches tall. But when another player quit in the middle of a game, Barkley got his chance. Coach Coupland made him a starter. For the rest of the season he averaged 13 points and 11 rebounds a game.

But the star that year was Travis Abernathy, Barkley's cousin. He had been a varsity starter since he was a freshman. By his senior season, he was one of the best players in Alabama. College coaches came to the Leeds games and practices to look him over and try to convince him to play for them. One day at practice Charles noticed Herbert Green, an assistant coach from Auburn University, watching his cousin. Barkley introduced himself and shook the coach's hand. "You know, we've got another pretty good guy on this team: me. I like Auburn. I wouldn't mind going to school there."[20] Green smiled, and probably forgot about Charles right away. After all, major colleges don't waste their time recruiting chubby high school players who are only five feet ten inches tall.

But after his junior year, Charles started growing. By the time his senior season started, he was six feet two inches tall. All the running, jumping, and shooting were starting to pay off. Now he was tall enough to compete with the "big boys." Late in the season he got his first dunk. He was stunned when he went up and slammed it through. He was also very happy that he had spent all those hours jumping over the chain-link fence.

There were other good players on the Leeds team, and they all liked to shoot. "The only way I was going to get to shoot the ball was if I got the rebound myself and put it back up," Barkley said.[21] So one night he grabbed 30 rebounds. He finished his senior season with an average of 19 points and 18 rebounds a game. By the end of the year, he was a star, and Leeds finished with a 26–3 record.

During the season, the team competed in a tournament in Birmingham, Alabama. Since many other fine teams were playing, too, the stands were filled with college coaches looking for talented players. Once again none of them was too interested in Barkley. They wanted to sign Bobby Lee Hurt, a six-foot-nine-inch center they figured was the best high school player in Alabama.

But then Hurt ran into Barkley. Charles used his jumping ability to block several shots and grab 20 rebounds. He also outscored the hotshot center 25–20. Suddenly, he was the center of attention. Coach Green had seen the game and wished he had paid more attention to Charles when he had met him the previous year at practice. Now nobody was laughing at Barkley's plans for a college scholarship and a career in the NBA.

Hurt got a scholarship to attend the University of Alabama, and Charles got one from Auburn. His impossible dream was starting to come true.

Chapter 3

Getting Motivated

Right away, head coach Sonny Smith knew Charles Barkley wasn't going to be like any of his other players at Auburn University.

His assistant, Herb Green, had told him about the talented boy from Leeds. They were afraid that sometimes during games he worked just hard enough to win. If his team was ahead, he liked to take it easy. He also looked a little chubby. But Smith didn't expect any special problems with Charles. He had worked with athletes for years. It wouldn't take long, he figured, to whip Charles into shape.

When Barkley came to Auburn for a visit, he didn't want to look over the campus. He just stayed at Smith's house, talking to the coach and his wife and watching television. During their talk, Smith

Since childhood, Barkley has been in a constant battle to keep off weight. In the NBA, where most players are tall and relatively thin, heavier players are at a disadvantage.

FACT

Most basketball teams exaggerate the heights of their players. During his career, Charles Barkley has been officially listed in game programs and rosters as six feet five inches or six feet six inches tall. But, as he himself has admitted, he's really only six feet four inches.

got a look at his new recruit's appetite. Charles ate two jars of green olives.

As a senior at Leeds High School, Barkley weighed 225 pounds. By the time he got to Auburn though, he had ballooned to 250. Smith told him to lose some weight, but Charles told him not to worry. He would play well no matter what he weighed. Then when the coach thought he was loafing at practice, Charles again told him not to worry. When it was important, when they were playing a game, he would play hard.

But Smith did worry. He didn't like Barkley's weight or his attitude. He made him run up and down the steps of the arena and around and around the court. Charles did the laps, but he didn't lose the weight, and he still didn't push himself at practice. Finally the coach was fed up. "You're not gonna start," he said, ". . . unless you practice hard."[1] Charles was fed up, too. He left the gym and went home to Leeds.

His mother was not happy to see him. She sent him back to Auburn. He had to return, she said, and at least finish his first year. This was his only chance to get a college education, and she was not going to let him blow it.

So Charles went back, but he continued to frustrate his coach. He was no longer a shy, quiet person. Now he wasn't afraid to say—and do—what he pleased. Smith had told his players never to snap the breakaway rims when they were practicing their dunks. Charles loved to dunk, and he thought it was fun to snap the rims. Finally the coach told him he'd be thrown out of practice if he snapped the rim again. Of course, Charles headed right for the basket for another dunk. Snap! Smith chased him from the arena.

Once Charles dunked the ball so hard in practice, he moved the backboard and its metal support out of place. Smith was furious. He figured it would take the whole team to get the basket back in place. After all, it was held in place by a pair of 300-pound cement blocks. Barkley just picked up the blocks, put the basket back where it belonged, and replaced the blocks.

One of the toughest things about college basketball for Charles was learning to lose. In his two years on the varsity team, Leeds High School had lost only ten games—and he had cried after each one. After his first defeat with Auburn, he sat in the locker room and cried again. His teammates told him to knock it off. "Man, you'd better not be crying around here after every loss," one of them said. "You'll flood us out of here."[2]

Of course, Barkley didn't always feel like crying.

In a game against Georgetown, he surprised Patrick Ewing by blocking one of his shots. How had he done that, the fans wondered. Wasn't Ewing seven inches taller? None of them knew about the chain-link fence around the house in Leeds. Playing against the nationally-ranked Hoyas, Charles got 24 points and 16 rebounds.

Then he ran into Bobby Lee Hurt, his old high school rival. By then, Hurt was a star for the Crimson Tide of Alabama, but he still remembered what Barkley had done to him in high school. Late in the game with the score tied, Hurt humiliated Charles by jumping over him and jamming the ball through the hoop.

Barkley didn't say anything, but the next time he touched the ball, he went up and over Bobby Lee to crash a dunk of his own. He also was fouled. As he walked to the free-throw line, he stuck a finger in Hurt's face. He wanted to make sure he got the message: *Don't mess with Charles Barkley!*

In a game against LSU, he stole a pass, dribbled through a pair of defenders, then slammed a dunk as he was fouled. This time as he waited for his free throw, he did a little dance of celebration.

The kid from Leeds began to attract the attention of fans across the country. Smith was happy that his difficult star was making people notice Auburn. The college's sports information department even

Sonny Smith, the Auburn basketball coach, tried to get Charles to lose weight and practice harder. Charles did lose the weight, but he and Smith still had trouble seeing eye-to-eye.

FACT

In the early 1980s, Charles Barkley and Bo Jackson were the biggest sports stars at Auburn University. Jackson won the Heisman Trophy in 1985 as a running back for the Tigers' football team. After college, he played baseball for the Kansas City Royals and football for the Los Angeles Raiders.

generated publicity by drawing attention to Charles's weight problem. They gave him some interesting nicknames: "Wide Load from Leeds," "Square Bear of Mid-Air," "Leaning Tower of Pizza," "Round Mound of Rebound," "Ton of Fun," and "Mouth of the South." Charles went along with the joke:

Why did he eat three whole chickens before a basketball game? "To make sure I wouldn't get hungry."

How did he lose weight? "Cut down to six meals a day."[3]

But after a while the joke got kind of old. "People concentrated on how much I weighed, not on how well I played," he said. "I led the conference in rebounding for three years, but nobody knew it. I was just a fat guy who could play basketball well."[4]

The statistics Barkley was piling up at Auburn were no joke. During his three seasons with the Tigers (1981–84), he got 1,183 points and 806 rebounds. That's 14.1 points and 9.6 rebounds per game.

Nobody seemed to enjoy rebounding like Charles. As he said later, "I don't want to lead the league in scoring . . . The only individual statistics I really care about are rebounds and assists."[5]

At the end of his junior year, Auburn lost the Southeastern Conference (SEC) championship in

Nashville, Tennessee. Charles was heartbroken. He sat on the floor of the arena and cried for five minutes. This time nobody tried to stop him.

Then in the first round of the NCAA postseason tournament, the Tigers played the Richmond Spiders. It was supposed to be an easy game, and everybody took it easy but the Spiders. With Charles playing a lazy game, usually not even bothering to cover his man, Richmond led 39–22 at the half.

Then Barkley and the Tigers woke up. Charles had a great second half, but the effort came too late and Auburn lost 72–71. Almost all the Tigers cried after the game. Their season was over, and they had blown a chance to be national champions.

Charles had another reason to cry. He had already decided he was leaving college basketball and heading for the NBA. What would the pro scouts think now, after his awful performance against Richmond? Would they figure he was a lazy player who choked in the big games?

Barkley wished he and the Tigers had another shot at the Spiders. But it was too late. It was time to say good-bye to Coach Smith and Auburn University.

Chapter 4

Rookie

Before he became a pro, Charles Barkley decided to try out for the 1984 Olympic team. The coach was Bobby Knight, the hot-tempered basketball genius from Indiana University.

Barkley and Knight didn't get along. "I didn't want to play for him," Charles said. "I didn't like the fact he was screaming at players all the time."[1]

The coach didn't like the big guard from Auburn, either. Knight thought he was too heavy and that he didn't work hard enough in practice. There was no doubt that Barkley was heavy, but it was obvious to most of the other players at tryouts that his weight didn't stop him from doing the job. Even at 284 pounds, he was one of the fastest men on the court.

Joe Dumars was also trying to make the Olympic

team. At one practice, Charles raced down the court on his way to what he figured would be a crashing slam dunk. But Dumars wanted to impress Knight, so he stepped in front of Barkley. Crash! Charles didn't make the shot. Instead, he ran over Dumars. Suddenly the gym was quiet. Dumars looked like the victim of a hit-and-run accident. He was still shaking and wheezing when Charles helped him to his feet. Even before he was up, he had decided he wouldn't take any more charges from Charles Barkley.

It didn't matter how many players he ran over. Barkley didn't make the American team. Knight didn't want him. Charles relaxed and waited to begin playing basketball as a professional in the NBA. The Philadelpia 76ers made him the fifth player chosen in the 1984 draft.

The 76ers were one of the finest teams in the league. They had won the championship two years before, and their 52–30 record was the third best for the 1983-84 season. Their biggest star was Julius Erving, one of the greatest forwards ever to play the game. The "Doctor" was known for his graceful flying dunks and hard work. Philadelphia's center was another veteran, Moses Malone, the NBA's leading rebounder for six seasons. Bobby Jones was the other forward. Andrew Toney and Maurice Cheeks played guard.

FACT

Bobby Knight is one of the most successful coaches in the NCAA. His teams at Indiana University won NCAA championships in 1976, 1981, and 1987. Even without Barkley, the 1984 United States Olympic team, which he coached, won the gold medal.

As a rookie with the Philadelphia 76ers, Barkley decided to work hard and lie low.

"Hey, fathead, welcome to the team!" was the way Malone greeted their new star.[2] Charles wasn't insulted by the name. For a while, at least, he decided to keep his mouth shut, work hard, and prove that he deserved to be on the team.

Being a professional basketball player is much different from playing in college. There are many more games—eighty-two in the NBA regular season. "I was on empty myself . . . after about thirty games during the 1984-85 season," Charles said.[3] And he still had three months to go!

If it hadn't been for Malone, Barkley might not have made it through his rookie season. The veteran center gave him advice. Stay tough, work at staying in shape, he told him, or you'll run out of gas before the season is over. When Charles was in a nasty mood, Moses told him a joke. When Charles needed praise, Moses was the one who gave him a pat on the back. Barkley said, "Obviously, Moses was the most influential person in my basketball career. Moses taught me not to trust anybody, to work hard, not to worry about hype, the fans, the media. He said to be my own man because nobody else will be there when push came to shove. I call Moses 'Dad.'"[4]

Malone also helped him listen to Billy Cunningham, the Philadelphia coach. Barkley still didn't like being yelled at. He also didn't enjoy being told what to

FACT

The Philadelphia 76ers made it to the NBA Finals in 1980 and 1982, but both times Kareem Abdul-Jabbar and Magic Johnson and the rest of the Los Angeles Lakers defeated them, 4 games to 2. In 1983, when the two teams met again for the title, Julius Erving and Moses Malone led the Philadelphia 76ers to a four-game sweep.

do. "I thought Cunningham was too tough on me in the beginning, so I rebelled," he said. "But I was immature and didn't understand what he was trying to do."[5]

The 76er fans didn't seem to mind his immaturity. They enjoyed his flashy style. On his 22nd birthday, Charles delivered a vicious "gorilla dunk" at the Spectrum in Philadelphia. By the time the ball hit the floor, the backboard and the 2,240-pound metal support behind it had moved six inches across the floor. A spokesman for the arena said, "The last time that support was moved it was by forklift."[6]

Midway through his first season, Charles became a starter. His teammates and the fans seemed to forget he was still a rookie. By the end of the season, he was averaging 14 points and 8.6 rebounds a game. The 76ers finished second in the Atlantic Division with a 58–24 record, the fourth best in the league. They beat the Washington Bullets in the first round of the postseason playoffs.

Then in the third game against the Milwaukee Bucks, Charles caught fire. After the Bucks took an early lead, he dropped in a pair of three-pointers and stole the ball twice. By then, he had become an expert at intimidation. When Milwaukee's Paul Mokeski attempted a layup, Charles dropped him

FACT

Julius Erving was one of the NBA's most popular players. "Dr. J." was known for his exciting, high-flying dunks. He played for the Virginia Squires and New York Nets in the old American Basketball Association before moving to the NBA and the 76ers. When Erving retired he had 18,364 points and a 22-points-per-game average.

on the court with a rough foul. Mokeski stayed away from Barkley—and the basket—the rest of the night. When the game was over, Charles had 19 points, 7 rebounds, and 5 blocked shots. Philadelphia won, 109-104.

After beating the Bucks, the 76ers finally fell to the Boston Celtics, four games to one, in the Eastern Conference Finals.

By then, Charles Barkley was a rich man. In October 1984, he had signed a contract with Philadelphia that would pay him $2 million over the next four years. As soon as he got his first check, he went on a wild spending spree. Within a few months he had spent $500,000 on cars, including a pair of Porsches, a BMW, and four luxury cars by Mercedes-Benz. He blew $10,000 a month just on food and entertainment.

But nobody could say he was selfish. He told his family they would never again have to worry about money. He bought a satellite dish for his grandmother so she could watch his games.

Barkley didn't just sit around all day and do nothing that summer, either. For the first time in several years, he spent his off-season practicing. He had listened to Malone, and he wanted to be in shape for the 1985–86 season. Maybe this would be the year the 76ers could knock off the Celtics

Halfway through his rookie season, Barkley earned a spot on the Sixers' starting lineup.

and the Los Angeles Lakers and take the NBA championship.

But the 76ers got off to a 5–8 start. They'd be lucky to get into the playoffs, let alone win the title. Barkley was mad. It seemed to him that not all his teammates were as interested in winning as he was. "I push myself unbelievably hard, and I expect perfection," he said. "If we lose and I say, 'Oh, it's just one game in 82,' then I'm a jerk. I've become a jerk just like everybody else. And I don't want to be like anybody else. I want to be special."[7]

Charles didn't want the 76ers to play like a bunch of jerks, so he convinced his teammates they should have a meeting and talk about their poor performance. Erving, the superstar, surprised Barkley by telling him to lead the discussion, so Charles took over. He asked each player to describe the team's problems. Some were angry that they weren't getting enough playing time. Others thought the starters were dogging it. The discussion seemed to clear the air. Suddenly the 76ers began playing well. They won nine straight games.

In a game against the Celtics, Barkley had 26 points and 21 rebounds. The Boston Garden crowd didn't enjoy his dunks, his intimidating tactics, or his smooth moves with the basketball. On one

Not only did the 76ers get knocked out of the playoffs in 1985, they also lost their star player, Moses Malone.

court-long race to the basket, he dribbled behind his back twice, once from each side.

Late in the regular season, Malone injured his eye, but the 76ers once again had the NBA's fourth-best record, 54–28. Barkley's 20-points-per-game scoring average was just 3.8 behind Moses, the team leader. As a rebounder with 12.8 rebounds per game, he was second only to Detroit's Bill Laimbeer, the league leader.

Playing without the injured Malone, the 76ers edged out Washington 3 games to 2 in the playoffs before falling to the Bucks in a seven-game series. In that series, Charles felt like he was facing Milwaukee's three seven-footers—Paul Mokeski, Randy Breuer, and Alton Lister—by himself. But he averaged 28 points and 15 rebounds a game. Despite his best efforts, Philadelphia dropped the deciding seventh game 113–112. Barkley and a lot of 76er fans figured the outcome would have been far different if Moses had been able to play. But as they watched the Celtics whip the Bucks and then the Houston Rockets for the title, there was nothing to do but wait until next year. By then, Malone's eye would be healed, and Philadelphia would have a real shot at the title.

But next year Moses was gone. The 76ers traded away the man Barkley called "Dad." It was, he said, "one of the saddest days of my life."[8]

Chapter 5

A Troubled Team

Moses Malone was gone. The 76ers had traded him and Terry Catledge to the Washington Bullets for Jeff Ruland and Cliff Robinson. It was a terrible trade. Not only was Moses Charles Barkley's best friend, he still had a few good seasons left. Ruland had a bad knee and played only five games for Philadelphia.

Andrew Toney, the Sixers' star guard, was soon hobbled by injuries, and he retired. Julius Erving, the team's superstar, announced that he, too, would retire after the 1986–87 season. It seemed to Charles that his team was falling apart.

On the same day they got rid of Malone, the 76ers traded their number one pick in the coming NBA draft to the Cleveland Cavs for Roy Hinson. If

Charles Barkley shows his frustration. Despite his spectacular performances, the 76ers were having terrible seasons.

they had kept the pick, they could have chosen Brad Daugherty, a seven-footer from the University of North Carolina.

Charles couldn't believe it. Barkley, Malone, Daugherty—what a team they might have been. Instead, it seemed to him, the Philadelphia front office had wrecked the team.

But Barkley was still in town, and he did what he could to make the team a winner. After his rookie season, his scoring average went up each year, from 14.0 to 20.0 to 23.0 to 28.3. In 1986–87, his third season, he became the shortest man in the history of the NBA to take the league rebounding championship. Fans wanted to know how a six-foot-four-inch guy could grab 14.6 rebounds a game.

But Charles's fine statistics weren't translating into success for the Sixers. In 1986–87, their record sank to 45–37, and they were eliminated by the Milwaukee Bucks in the first round of the playoffs. The next season they were 36–46 and didn't even qualify for postseason play. In 1988–89, Barkley was named team captain and finished second in the league rebounding stats. That helped lead the 76ers to a 46–36 record, but they were blanked three games to none in the playoffs by the New York Knicks.

It was a disappointing time to be in Philadelphia,

but Charles tried to make the best of it. He gave his all every time he stepped on the court. Down by 2 points with time running out against the Charlotte Hornets, he charged down the lane for a layup. Bodies fell and so did the ball—right through the hoop. But as the Hornets picked themselves up off the court, Barkley was called for charging: no basket. Charlotte won 109–107.

He faced the same situation two nights later in Indiana. Charles didn't hesitate. He went for the basket again. It was good! This time the Pacers were called for the foul. Barkley sank the free throw, and Philadelphia had a three-point lead and eventually a victory.

Against the Portland Trail Blazers, he had some fun with Mark Bryant, their rookie center. When Bryant got the ball, Charles stood apart from the rest of the players, waved his arms and yelled, "Yo!" The trick worked. Bryant threw the ball right to him. That wasn't all he did to Portland that night. He also brought down 22 rebounds.

By then Barkley had realized he wasn't playing basketball just for fun. "I love basketball," he said, "but I wouldn't do this unless I was making money. My knees, ankles and back hurt so much I wonder, 'Is it worth it?'"[1] His arms were covered with scratches and scars. Every night he was pushed, elbowed, and bumped. It wasn't easy being a pro in the NBA.

Scratches and bruises are one thing, permanent damage is another. On November 4, 1986, Charles reached for a rebound but fell, slamming his body onto the floor. "The pain of that injury was the worst that I've ever felt because I couldn't escape it," he said. "It hurt when I breathed, which meant it hurt all the time."[2]

Barkley had damaged his spleen, a purple organ about the size of a fist. From its spot in the abdomen just behind the stomach, it filters blood and helps fight infection. Charles must have hit the floor pretty hard, because his spleen was ruptured, or ripped open.

Several doctors told him the spleen would have to be taken out in an operation. That would mean he would probably miss most of the rest of the season. But Charles got lucky. Before he had surgery, he went to Dr. Julie Grosh, a spleen expert. Maybe, she said, he could keep his spleen. If he just rested for a few weeks, it might heal itself.

Dr. Grosh was right. Barkley sat out for nine games before returning to action. His spleen healed and hasn't given him any more problems.

Charles was being well paid for his efforts and his pain. In 1986, he had signed a long-term contract with the Sixers that would pay him an average of $1.5 million a year. With various bonuses figured in, the contract was worth $12 million. At the same time, he was earning $500,000 for doing Nike commercials.

Of course, Barkley liked the money, but what he really wanted was a championship. In fact, he wanted it so much, he was even willing to help pay for it. Under NBA rules, there's a limit to how much a team can pay its players. Charles offered to give $250,000 back to the Sixers so the team could hire better players. The Sixers thanked him, but turned down his offer.

In 1987, Charles met his wife, Maureen, in a restaurant. She was a pretty blonde woman, and he convinced her friend to give him her phone number. Of course, she recognized him right away. It seemed that everybody in Philadelphia knew Charles Barkley. After watching him for years on television, Maureen had figured he was probably a jerk. When she talked to him, though, she was surprised because he was so polite.

Over the next few months, Charles was able to convince her that he was really a pretty nice guy, and they were married. Then on May 15, 1989, their daughter, Christiana, was born. Right from the start, Barkley enjoyed being a father. He plastered her pictures all over his locker and loved to play with her. Most fans would have been surprised watching this big man with the mean reputation teaching his little baby how to head-butt.

In 1989, the 76ers signed Johnny Dawkins, a fine young guard, and Rick Mahorn, one of the toughest "Bad Boys" from the championship Detroit Pistons. For the first time in years, it looked like Philadelphia had the players to take a shot at the NBA title.

Early in the 1989–90 season, Charles challenged his team to win ten straight games, then celebrate by having their ears pierced. The 76ers won the games, and many of them were soon wearing earrings. Off court, Charles almost always wore a diamond stud in his right ear.

The most memorable game of the season probably came on April 19, 1990, when the Sixers whipped the Pistons. With time running out, Isiah Thomas took a swing at his old teammate Mahorn. After Thomas was ejected from the game, Mahorn slam-dunked the ball, giving Philadelphia a 105–95 lead. But then Piston Bill Laimbeer grabbed the ball and rubbed it in Mahorn's face. That was too much for Charles. He punched Laimbeer twice and soon there was a pile of players on the floor slugging it out. Nobody was hurt, but the league handed out $162,500 in fines. The fight cost Barkley a one-game suspension and $51,700. But his message was clear: *Don't mess with my teammates.*

For the first time in years, it looked as though Philadelphia might have a chance in the playoffs.

By 1990, there was no doubt that Charles was a superstar. He was one of the richest, best-known athletes in the world. His 1989–90 rebounding average of 11.5 made him third in the league. He also averaged 25.2 points per game. He was the man who carried Philadelphia to a 53–29 record and first place in the Atlantic Division. Some Sixers fans hoped those statistics would help him win the league's Most Valuable Player award. But in the closest finish ever, Michael Jordan got the honor. Charles figured he would never be MVP. He was too loud and too bold, and too many people thought he was a jerk. Besides, as he had already said, "I know I'm one of the best players in the league. I can play with anybody. I don't need the MVP to tell me that."[3]

In the 1990 playoffs, Philadelphia slipped by the Cavs three games to two. Then they were destroyed by Jordan and the Chicago Bulls, winning just one game out of five. It was obvious that the Sixers weren't ready yet to take a championship from the really great teams in the league. Once more the season ended in frustration.

After the 1989–90 season, Charles Barkley didn't have much fun in Philadelphia. Johnny Dawkins and Rick Mahorn missed a lot of action because of injuries. Some of the other 76ers played like they

In spite of the 76ers' losses, Barkley was considered by most fans to be a great player. In 1990 he lost to Michael Jordan in MVP voting in the closest margin ever.

didn't really care how the games turned out. Barkley was tired. "I couldn't carry the load by myself any longer . . ." he said. "My teammates played like I was supposed to do it all every night."[4]

His scoring average rose to 27.6 in 1990–91, the second-best total of his career, but his rebounds were down to 10.1. The Sixers' record fell to 44–38. In the playoffs they blanked Milwaukee, but again got whipped in five games by the Bulls.

The next season was worse. Two months into it, Charles noticed "my teammates stopped giving me the kind of support I needed in order for us to be a strong team . . . We were becoming more and more of a one-man show."[5]

How much longer would the frustration go on? Would the 76ers ever be a championship-caliber team? Charles's time was running out. He had already invested six years of his career in Philadelphia. With the beating his body was taking, he didn't figure he had many good years left.

If he couldn't win in Philadelphia, what were his chances of going someplace else? Some teams had talked about trading high draft picks and fine young players for Barkley, but the Sixers said no. It looked as if Barkley was stuck in Philadelphia.

Chapter 6

Bad Luck

Besides being unhappy in Philadelphia, Charles Barkley was usually in a great deal of pain. By 1992, he was a twenty-nine-year-old athlete in his sixteenth season of basketball. His body didn't recover as quickly as it used to from bumps and bruises, and the serious injuries seemed to hurt even more.

One of the worst came in 1989 when he went up for a rebound. Bump! Another player slammed into his shoulder, and it hurt. But he didn't leave the court. He kept playing. When it kept hurting in the days that followed, he still kept playing. After each game, he covered it with ice to numb the pain. He told himself it was just a bruise.

But the pain was still there when the season ended. All summer long he tried to fix the injury himself by lifting weights to strengthen the shoulder. When that didn't work, he finally told the team doctor. After the examination, the doctor told him he wasn't surprised the shoulder hurt. The muscle wasn't bruised. It was ruptured. There were only two ways to fix it—rest or surgery.

But the 1989–90 season was about to start. Charles said he had no time for rest or surgery. He would play and continue icing the shoulder after practices and games. After the season, there would be time to rest or to have an operation. For months he would have to play in intense pain. By the end of the season, each time he shot, it felt like a knife had been stabbed into his shoulder.

Finally, on June 25, 1990, he underwent surgery to repair the muscle. After weeks of physical therapy and exercise, he was ready for the 1990–91 season.

On March 31, 1991, Charles forgot all about the old injury in his shoulder. He was struggling for a rebound against the Cleveland Cavaliers when Rick Mahorn lost his balance and fell backwards, right on Charles.

Snap!

Barkley grabbed his left knee and fell to the floor. As the crowd in the Spectrum fell silent, he screamed. He was in terrible pain.

When he was helped off the floor, he couldn't

put any weight on the leg. He was scared that the collision had ripped all the tendons, ligaments, and muscles in the knee. He feared he would never play basketball again. He wondered if he would even be able to walk again.

Barkley's wife, Maureen, and his grandmother watched as he was taken from the arena. They were with him in the locker room when the team doctor examined him. All three of them were surprised by the good news.

The knee was sprained, not broken, and the ligaments were torn. The doctor told him he could be playing again in a month. Two weeks later, Charles was back on the court.

On January 11, 1992, Barkley went up and came down awkwardly, his left foot landing on teammate Hersey Hawkins.

Pop!

This time the pain was in his ankle. As he hobbled to the bench, he hoped it wasn't broken. Once again, he was lucky. The pain was caused not by a break, but by three stress fractures, or tiny cracks, in the bone. After three weeks, the ankle still hurt, but he was once again back on the court.

Of course, just because Charles was playing again didn't mean his problems were over. The Sixers still weren't winning as much as he would

Charles has had more than his share of troubles—injuries, an arrest on gun charges, and a major controversy over a fight with a heckler.

have liked. And he seemed to have just as many problems off the court.

Back on August 17, 1988, he was stopped by a state trooper near Atlantic City, New Jersey, for speeding. When the officer checked his '88 black Porsche, she found a loaded handgun lying on the back seat. Charles had a permit to carry the gun in Pennsylvania, but not in New Jersey. He was arrested and briefly taken to jail.

Barkley never said he thought he deserved special treatment because he was a celebrity. When he had trouble, he said, "I accept it like a man. 'Hey, I messed up, bring the heat in. I just have to deal with it.'"[1] He didn't have to deal with the gun charges for long. Within a few weeks, a judge dismissed them. There was no reason, he said, for the trooper to search his car in the first place.

The worst part about being a celebrity, Charles thought, was putting up with all the jerks who tried to show off by showing him up in public. "You've got people who go out and get drunk and they've got liquid courage, and they want to make a scene, so they punch Charles Barkley, or they say, 'Charles Barkley punched me in the face—how much am I going to sue him for?'"[2]

In December 1991, he got into a fight with a man outside a restaurant in Milwaukee. The man harassed

Charles while he was eating, then followed him to his car. After yelling more insults, the man challenged him to a fight. So Charles punched him in the nose—and broke it.

Reporters wondered why Barkley didn't stay away from public places and avoid the few crazy fans. He said he didn't want trouble. In a fight with a fan, there was no way he could win. Either he would be a wimp for refusing to throw a punch or a bully for beating the guy up. "But I'm not going to stay in the house all the time. I mean, this is the best time of my life. I'm going to enjoy it."[3]

By the time Charles punched the man outside the restaurant, many people already were sure he was the one who was the jerk. It wasn't just his rough style of play; or the way he yelled and complained on the court; or the crazy things he sometimes said to reporters. It was because on March 26, 1991, he spit on a little girl.

It was late at the Meadowlands, the home court of the New Jersey Nets. Throughout the game, a loud fan in the front row had been yelling racial slurs at Charles. While he was watching a free throw, Barkley spat at the man. He missed the man and hit Lauren Rose, an 8-year-old girl sitting with her parents near the vulgar fan.

What kind of a jerk spits on a little girl? Charles

was ashamed and horrified. So were league officials. They suspended him for a game and fined him $10,000.

Barkley called Lauren and apologized to her and her father. "For once, I was sorry for something I had done on the basketball court," he said.[4] He quietly bought the Rose family season tickets for the next year's Nets games. He also invited them to a banquet. The Roses accepted his apology and told him they knew he hadn't meant to spit on the little girl.

Charles wasn't accustomed to apologizing, and he hardly ever thinks he's wrong, but the spitting incident was different. "That was a major, major, *major* occurrence in Charles's life," said Maureen almost four years later. "It just eats him alive. Still."[5]

"What does that say about me, that I let a basketball game—a game!—get to me so much that I want to spit on any other human being? It was my fault. It was me. It was all me. After that I started to become a better person."[6]

Actually, Charles has always had a soft spot in his heart for kids. A few years later, after a terrible game, he stormed back to his locker just as a teammate's young sons walked into the locker room. "I'm in a bad mood!" he screamed at them. "I want to bite somebody's head off! How about you?!"

"No!" yelled the five-year-old.

Barkley turned to the boy's three-year-old brother. "Do you want me to eat you?"

"No!" the boy screamed back at him. "I'm going to eat you!" Charles smiled and turned to his locker. Taped to the door were five pictures of his daughter Christiana.

Another time, he met a four-year-old girl in a hotel lobby. "Are you Charles Barkley?" she asked.

"Yes, I am."

"Are you mean?"

"Not till seven-thirty P.M."[7] [Game time.]

Late in 1993, he visited ten-year-old Jason Silva in a Tucson, Arizona, hospital where he was dying of Hodgkin's disease. That night Charles wore a white band with two letters that he wouldn't explain: JS. Watching on the hospital television, Jason recognized his initials. In the game, Barkley had 35 points, his best total so far that season.

Even though he has been offered thousands of dollars to sell his autographs, Barkley has always refused. His fans get them for free.

But all the free autographs in the world couldn't change the way the Philadelphia 76ers were playing in the 1991–92 season. "We stunk," Charles said. "Management wasn't trying to win. I was like Custer back there, riding into the massacre every night."[8] Despite Barkley's 23.1 points and 11.1

Although Barkley continued to turn in star performances, the 76ers were not serious contenders for the NBA championship.

rebounds per game, Philadelphia's miserable 35–47 record didn't even earn a spot in the playoffs. "It's no fun going to work every night and getting your brains beat out."[9]

Again there was some talk about Charles being traded to another team, but hardly anybody believed a deal could be put together. Any team that wanted Barkley would have to give up two or three good players to get him.

On June 17, 1992, Barkley started having fun again. He was in Milwaukee for his trial on charges brought against him by the fan he had slugged six months before. The jury decided he was innocent. They figured he hadn't started the fight. The other man had provoked him, and it wasn't Charles's fault.

The verdict was just the start of good things. As he waited to board his plane back to Philadelphia, he called the Sixers' office. He had been traded! The Phoenix Suns had traded three players—Jeff Hornacek, Andrew Lang, and Tim Perry—to get him.

Barkley bought a drink for everybody on the plane and smiled all the way home.

Chapter 7

Olympic Hero and MVP

Charles Barkley did his best not to sound like a jerk when he left Philadelphia for Phoenix. "I love Philadelphia and I love the Sixers. I'd have done anything for the Sixers," he said.[1] But, he figured, it was time for him to go.

Before he joined the Suns he spent the summer of 1992 playing on the United States Olympic basketball squad. With players like Barkley, Michael Jordan, Larry Bird, Magic Johnson, Patrick Ewing, and Clyde Drexler, it was easy to see why it was called the Dream Team. Many fans figured it was the greatest basketball team of all time.

"I know a lot of people would give their right arm and leg to be on this team," Charles said. "This is a great feeling. Being on this team is so much

FACT

The 1992 Dream Team was made up of Charles Barkley, Clyde Drexler, Larry Bird, Patrick Ewing, Magic Johnson, Michael Jordan, Christian Laettner, Karl Malone, Chris Mullin, Scottie Pippen, David Robinson, and John Stockton. Ewing, Jordan, and Mullin also played on the winning 1984 team.

fun."[2] The Dream Team would be competing against squads from all over the world at the Olympic Games in Barcelona, Spain.

Some opposing players said they weren't worried about playing against Barkley and the American team. "That's all right," Charles chuckled. "All I have to say is they better be ready to play against us. If we come out and play the way we're capable, they're in trouble."[3]

He was right. The other teams were in trouble. The Americans outscored their eight opponents by an average of 43.8 points per game and coasted to Olympic gold medals. Barkley led the Dream Team in points. Sportswriters praised him for a great performance. "It was like they suddenly discovered I was good," he said. "I'd always been good."[4]

Then it was time to join his new team. Phoenix was about to become the home of one of the most exciting basketball players in the world.

The Suns fans were happy to learn that on the basketball court, Barkley was still not a nice guy. He screamed, he growled, he pushed, and he ran over people. "When he leans on you," said Robert Parrish of the Charlotte Hornets, "it's like being crushed by a trash compactor."[5]

Charles wants his opponents to believe he's a wild man. "He thinks that gives him an edge," said his wife Maureen. "He thinks it intimidates people."[6]

"My strategy is simple," Barkley wrote in his autobiography *Outrageous!* "I try to beat up anybody I play against hoping that when the fourth quarter arrives, they'll have nothing left."[7]

Of course, he didn't have any doubts about his ability: "God just made me special and that's the only way you can look at it," he said. "There will never be another 6' 4" guy who can accomplish what I've accomplished. Ever. Ever."[8]

Behind the temper tantrums and the flagrant fouls, there was a friendly, caring man who liked to keep things neat and tidy. After tearing apart the basketball court, Barkley wanted his locker room and home spick-and-span. When a teammate tossed tape on the floor, Charles asked, "How long would it take you to walk over and put that in the trash?" He shook his head and sighed, "I'm living with animals."[9] Sometimes he relaxed after a game by vacuuming carpets or shining mirrors at his home. He brushed his teeth before every game.

Many of the players who were shoved and run over by big, bad Sir Charles would probably be surprised to learn that he has always had a very soft spot in his heart for his mother. "If loving and

Despite the change of uniform, Barkley's aggressive play still thrilled fans across the country.

respecting your mother and being proud of her makes you a mama's boy," he said, "then that's what I am."[10]

When Barkley was still a student at Auburn, he sent his mother a Christmas card with the message, "One of these days I'm gonna give you everything you ever wanted because you're the best mama in the world."[11] Charcey Glenn has stayed in the same house in Leeds, Alabama, but now it has another bedroom, a playroom, and an extra bathroom. The three-car garage is full of sports cars and luxury automobiles.

Whether he was playing in Philadelphia or Phoenix, Charles Barkley wasn't easy to figure out, but he was hard to ignore. And it was impossible not to notice how much fun he has been having ever since he got that transfusion at Leeds Hospital when he was a tiny baby. "Life's got to be funny," he has said. "If you're not enjoying it, you might as well be dead."[12]

On one of his first visits to Phoenix, Barkley was given a tour of the Suns' new arena by Cotton Fitzsimmons, the team's vice president. It was a beautiful facility, Fitzsimmons said, but not yet complete. "Look at the ceiling. See what's missing."[13] There was no championship banner.

Charles smiled. He knew what the Phoenix

Barkley was pleased with his move to Phoenix. The Suns were an up-and-coming team, ready to break into the playoffs.

Suns expected from him. "I'm not going to sit here and guarantee us a championship, but I think we've got a shot at it, and that's all anybody can ask."[14] He wanted everybody to know he was glad to be in Phoenix. "Now I've got help around me . . . Maybe I've lost a step. Maybe I'm not as quick as I used to be . . . But I'm still a pretty good basketball player."[15]

Barkley was good enough to win the 1992–93 Most Valuable Player award. He was good enough to take the Phoenix Suns to the NBA Finals. But once again, he was stopped short of a championship.

While he was having his great first year with his new team, Charles was attracting lots of attention off the basketball court, too. In an unusual television commercial for Nike, he said, "I am not a role model . . . I am paid to wreak havoc on the basketball court. Parents should be role models. Just because I dunk a basketball doesn't mean I should raise your kids."[16]

Many people didn't like the commercial. It seemed to them that Charles was just trying to excuse himself for his temper tantrums and other mistakes. But soon other people came to his defense. Why should athletes be role models? Shouldn't parents be the ones setting an example for their children?

FACT

The Phoenix Suns and Milwaukee Bucks joined the NBA as expansion teams in 1968. It took the Bucks only three seasons to win a league title. In the 1971 Finals, Kareem Abdul-Jabbar, then known as Lew Alcindor, led them to victory over the Baltimore Bullets. Until Barkley arrived, the Suns had appeared in only one NBA Final, losing in 1976 to the Boston Celtics.

FACT

Chris Evert was a star of women's tennis in the 1970s and 1980s. Monica Seles, Steffi Graf, and Zina Garrison are stars of women's tennis today. Track-and-field star Jackie Joyner-Kersee won the gold in the heptathalon event in the 1988 and 1992 Olympics.

Barkley said as a child he had been lucky to have two fine role models—"my mother and grandmother. They were the only people I looked up to and respected a great deal."[17]

As an adult, he felt a responsibility to be a role model only to his daughter Christiana: "Her mother and I are her role models. Not Michael Jordan . . . Not Chris Evert. Not Jackie Joyner-Kersee. Not Monica Seles, Steffi Graf, or Zina Garrison or any other female athlete. It's Charles and Maureen Barkley's job to raise their child, no one else's."[18]

He said kids spent too much time worrying about sports and making lots of money. Very, very few of them will ever be professional athletes. Only one out of every ten thousand high school basketball players will make it to the NBA. Young people should be more concerned with getting a good education and learning how to be decent, productive citizens. It is the job of their parents to help them.

By the time Barkley moved to Phoenix, Christiana was three years old. She and her mother remained in Philadelphia for a few months after her father moved to Phoenix. "She calls me every morning from Philly . . ." he said. "She goes, 'Daddy, did Phoenix win?' . . . She has to go to bed before our game is over . . . I hate telling her, 'Nah, Phoenix lost, baby. I'm sorry.'"[19]

Soon Maureen and Christiana joined Charles in Phoenix. He hoped that someday soon he would be able to take his little girl to the Suns' arena and show her the championship banner he had helped his team to win.

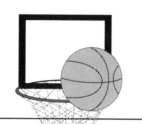

Chapter 8

One More Goal

Just before the start of the 1993–94 season, Charles Barkley decided his body couldn't take much more of the National Basketball Association. But he wanted to stick around long enough to take one more shot at the NBA championship. That's the way he wanted to end his career.

However, a torn quadriceps muscle and a swollen spinal disk kept him out of seventeen games. He played in only sixty-five regular season matches, his lowest professional total ever.

Barkley finished the season with an average of 21.6 points and 11.2 rebounds a game. That gave him the ninth best scoring average in the league. "You know how good I am?" he asked. "I'm the only player who can be in the top 10 in scoring and rebounding and be on a winning team and have people say I had a bad year."[1]

For several months, Charles was an impatient man. "I just want to get the regular season over," he kept saying.[2] When it was finally finished and Phoenix was assured a spot in the playoffs, he said, "Gonna be fun. . . . Ain't no better place to be than the playoffs."[3]

The Suns wiped out the Golden State Warriors in three straight games. The finale was an awesome display of Barkley at his best. He had 11 shots in a row without a miss and 27 points in the first quarter.

Charles played only sixty-five regular season games during the 1993–94 season due to a torn leg muscle and swollen spinal disk. In his tenth season in the NBA, his body was beginning to show the wear and tear of professional basketball.

"It was like God was letting me do it," he said.[4] Charles's 56 points led Phoenix to a 140–133 win.

In the second round, the Suns ran into Hakeem Olajuwon and the Houston Rockets. "Now we have to get ready to play against the best center in the world, and it ain't gonna be no fun ..." Barkley said. "We knew that the toughest series would be with Houston and that monster [Olajuwon] in the middle."[5]

Once again his back was giving him trouble. During the second game with Seattle, he had experienced spasms that made it hard to keep going. But, as he pointed out, "playing with pain is part of the game."[6]

In the opener against the Rockets, the Suns overcame an eighteen-point deficit to win, 91–87. Barkley had 34 points and 15 rebounds in Game 2, a 124–117 Phoenix victory.

Then the Rockets surprised almost everybody with a pair of victories and the series was tied. In those losses Charles missed 27 of 43 shots. Olajuwon easily batted away one of his dunks. Reporters wondered why he was playing so poorly. Was he hurt? Barkley wouldn't say. He refused to make excuses. "I'm not playing well. Leave it at that."[7]

But Charles *was* hurt. Besides the pain in his back, he also had a strained groin muscle that made it difficult to walk, let alone play basketball. Somehow, he still managed to score 30 points in Game 5, a 109–86 Houston victory. When Phoenix won the next game, 109–86, the stage was set for the climactic seventh game.

In that one, the Rockets were ahead by sixteen points until the Suns stormed back to within one, 77–76, late in the third quarter. But this time Houston played tough and never surrendered the lead. Olajuwon's dunk with 1:30 left made it 99–92, and that was the end of the line for Phoenix.

At home, Maureen Barkley watched on television. "I saw him kinda chugging along . . . The pain in his face . . . I was in tears . . . I couldn't stand to see him play."[8]

Just 7.4 seconds before the final buzzer, Hakeem was closing in on the basket for another dunk. Charles said no. He slammed into Olajuwon, picking up a foul. Vernon Maxwell, of the Rockets, didn't like to see his superstar roughed up, so he ran to Barkley. Charles was in no mood to talk, so he shoved Maxwell. Both players were thrown out of the game.

After the Houston victory, Charles didn't whine about his foul or being tossed out of the game. "I think the best team won this series," he said.[9] Reporters wondered if he was finished with basketball. "The bottom line is I'm not going to play with the pain I've been in. I'm going to get with the doctors and if they can make me better, fine. If not, it's been a great ride. It's strictly a medical decision. But I'm not going to torture myself again."[10]

His doctors told him there was a way to reduce the pain and continue his career. By stretching and exercising during the off-season he could strengthen his back so that most of the pain would disappear. When the time came to play basketball again, he was in great shape.

Why did he work so hard to keep playing? Was he planning on another MVP trophy? "I've got one," he said. "Another would only clutter my house. We're playing for a championship here, not MVP awards."[11]

But then in an exhibition game, he strained a muscle in his abdomen. The pain was so great he missed the first ten games of the season. He didn't play until November 26, 1994, against the San Antonio Spurs. When he finally hit the court, he wasn't in great shape. He wore a girdle to hold his abdominal muscles tight, but that didn't disguise the fact that he had gained ten pounds while waiting to heal. He looked sluggish moving up and down the floor, and he even shot a pair of air balls.

In the fourth quarter though, Barkley went to

FACT

Hakeem "The Dream" Olajuwon was born in Lagos, Nigeria. He was a soccer star until he switched to basketball when he was fifteen years old. He led the University of Houston to two NCAA title games, but never played on a championship team until the Houston Rockets beat the New York Knicks in the 1994 NBA Finals. A year later, the Rockets made it two in a row by winning the Finals against the Orlando Magic.

In 1994, Hakeem Olajuwon and the Houston Rockets defeated the Suns in the second round of the playoffs before going on to win their first NBA Championship.

Thanks to Charles Barkley, the Phoenix Suns are still a major force in the competitive Western Conference.

work. The Spurs tied the game 99–99 on a pair of free throws by David Robinson. That seemed to get Charles fired up. "I have a God-given ability to make plays when the game is on the line," he said. "It doesn't matter how bad I'm playing. I'm confident I'll always make the plays."[12] He made 10 points in the final quarter, and Phoenix won 111–108.

The Suns were first in the Pacific Division with a 59–23 record for 1994–95. Barkley averaged 23 points and 11.1 rebounds per game. Only Dennis Rodman, Dikembe Mutombo, and Shaquille O'Neal had better rebounding averages. Charles was also hot in the playoffs, averaging 25.7 points a game.

Unfortunately for the Suns, they didn't last long in the postseason. After shutting out Portland, three games to none, Phoenix jumped ahead of the defending champion Houston Rockets, three games to one. Just one more loss and the Rockets would be eliminated.

But, as Houston coach Rudy Tomjanovich proudly pointed out, "Never underestimate the heart of a champion."[13] Olajuwon and the Rockets won the last three games, ending the Suns' season. Then they took apart San Antonio and Orlando to earn their second straight NBA title.

Once again, Charles had to watch another team celebrate. However, he was still in the news thanks to a comment he had made earlier in the season. Way back in February, he was surprised by what he felt was a stupid question from a white reporter. "That's why I hate white people," he joked to another white reporter.[14]

Not everybody thought the joke was funny. "The NBA got, I think they told me, 6,000 calls in one day wanting to ban me," he said. He couldn't understand why people couldn't just laugh at his silly comment. "You can't say anything. You can't joke. It's always something."[15]

McDonald's Corporation thought Barkley was funny enough to hire him as their spokesman for a series of televisions commercials that began running the day after Christmas in 1995. In them, Charles pretended that he was having trouble repeating the restaurant's Big Mac slogan.

His success with commercials might be paving the way for a future career as a sports announcer. According to news reports, NBC TV was anxious to hire him as soon as his basketball career ended. [16]

Meanwhile Barkley was still playing basketball. Before the 1995–96 season, Coach Paul Westphal said a great effort from Charles and his teammates

No matter what Barkley decides to do after basketball, fans know it won't be done quietly.

"will give us a chance to compete for Phoenix's first NBA Championship."[17]

NBA championship or not, Charles Barkley knows he can't play basketball forever. What will he do when he finally retires? "I'm going to take up skiing," he said. "Who's going to think to look for a large black man on a ski slope?"[18]

If not skiing, how about another sport? "I love boxing best . . ." he said. "The money these guys make? I'd do that. I'd get in there with George Foreman, and I'd tell you, it'd all be over fast . . . I'd be knocked out for the right amount of money."[19]

Maybe he'll give up working with his body and concentrate on improving his mind. "I'm going to learn how to play the piano . . . and how to speak in sign language. Those are my goals."[20]

But does he really want to work that hard? At other times he's talked about relaxing. "I'm going down to Puerto Rico to hang out at the crap tables."[21] Gambling in a casino does seem a lot easier than basketball—or skiing or boxing.

Of course, sometimes Charles is just pulling our leg. Nobody really expects him to jump into the ring with Foreman—or any other boxer. One thing he seems to be serious about is politics. In 1994, he spent a day in Washington, D. C., talking to senators and Supreme Court justices. "This was my home-work," he said. "I'm preparing."[22]

Barkley spent four hours talking to Justice Clarence Thomas, and for once he was humble. "I think I'm smart, but I was learning on the go talking with him . . . He's achieved true greatness."[23]

But Charles doesn't plan on joining Thomas on the bench. In 1994, he said, "I'd like to go into politics and be the governor of Alabama four years from now."[24] He thinks he's the ideal man to run the state. "I won't be looking out for any particular group. I've been on both ends of the spectrum. I've been poor. I've been rich. Hopefully, I can do a good job."[25]

He's especially concerned with the young peo-ple of Alabama. "I would pop more money into the public school system . . . Also, we have to get tougher on crime. People are not afraid to commit crimes in our society today and that's wrong."[26]

Being Alabama's governor isn't the first political job Charles has thought about. Way back in 1984 when Auburn University was advertising him as "The Leaning Tower of Pizza," he announced, "My goal in life is to become President, lock up every-body over 12 and let kids rule the world."[27]

Chapter Notes

Chapter 1

1. Vern E. Smith and Aric Press, "Who You Calling Hero?," *Newsweek*, vol. 121, (May 24, 1993), p. 65.

2. Mike Tulumello, "Winning Title Is All That's Left for Barkley," *New York Times News Service*, May 1, 1994.

3. *Sir Charles,* Prod. NBA Entertainment. Videocassette. CBS Fox Video, 1994.

4. "Barkley and Suns Deep-Six the Spurs," *The New York Times*, (May 21, 1993), p. B17.

5. Tom Friend, "Barkley Leads Suns to Dreamers' Matchup," *The New York Times*, (June 6, 1983), sec. 8, p. 3.

6. Tom Friend, "Barkley Locates Knicks on Horizon," *The New York Times*, (May 27, 1993), p. B16.

7. *Sir Charles.*

8. Mark Vancil, "Bulls' three-peat was anything but easy," *The Sporting News NBA Guide*, (St. Louis: The Sporting News, 1993), p. 24.

9. Ibid., p. 26.

10. Ibid.

11. *Sir Charles.*

12. Frank Deford, "Barkley's Last Shot," *Vanity Fair*, vol. 58, (February 1995), p. 126.

Chapter 2

1. Bruce Newman, "A Double Feature All by Himself," *Sports Illustrated,* vol. 64, (March 24, 1986), p. 34.

2. Charles Moritz, *Current Biography Yearbook,* (New York: H.W. Wilson Company, 1991), p. 50.

3. Alan Richman, "Call Him 'Round Mound' at Your Peril; Charles Barkley's Bite is Worse Than His Woof," *People,* vol. 27, (April 27, 1987), p. 78.

4. "Ask Me Anything You Want!," *Sports Illustrated for Kids,* vol. 6, (May 1994), p. 53.

5. *Sir Charles,* Prod. NBA Entertainment. Videocassette. CBS Fox Video, 1994.

6. Ibid.

7. Moritz, p. 50.

8. Charles Barkley and Roy S. Johnson, *Outrageous!* (New York: Avon Books, 1992), p. 64.

9. Richman, p. 78.

10. *Sir Charles.*

11. Ibid.

12. David Casstevens, *Somebody's Gotta Be Me: The Wide, Wide World of the One & Only Charles Barkley,* (Kansas City, Mo.: Andrews & McMeel, 1994), p. 143.

13. Tom Friend, "What You See Isn't What Barkley Is," *The New York Times,* (May 30, 1993), sec. 8, p. 2.

14. Vern E. Smith and Aric Press, "Who You Calling Hero?," *Newsweek,* vol. 121, (May 24, 1993), p. 64.

15. *Sir Charles.*

16. Ibid.

17. Glen Macnow, *Sports Great Charles Barkley,* (Hillside, N.J.: Enslow Publishers, Inc., 1992), p. 18.

18. *Sir Charles.*

19. Newman, p. 34.

20. *Outrageous!*, p. 90.

21. Newman, p. 35.

Chapter 3

1. Charles Barkley and Roy S. Johnson, *Outrageous!* (New York: Avon Books, 1992), p. 100.

2. Ibid., p. 97.

3. Alexander Wolff, "The Leaning Tower of Pizza," *Sports Illustrated,* vol. 60, (March 12, 1984), p. 58.

4. Alan Richman, "Call Him 'Round Mound' at Your Peril; Charles Barkley's Bite is Worse Than His Woof," *People,* vol. 27, (April 27, 1987), p. 78.

5. Charles Barkley with Rick Reilly, *Sir Charles: The Wit and Wisdom of Charles Barkley,* (New York: Warner Books, 1994), p. 50.

Chapter 4

1. Bruce Newman, "A Double Feature All by Himself," *Sports Illustrated,* vol. 64, (March 24, 1986), p. 38.

2. Charles Barkley and Roy S. Johnson, *Outrageous!* (New York: Avon Books, 1992), p. 14.

3. Ibid., p. 168.

4. Charles Barkley with Rick Reilly, *Sir Charles: The Wit and Wisdom of Charles Barkley,* (New York: Warner Books, 1994), pp. 82–83.

5. Charles Moritz, *Current Biography Yearbook,* (New York: H.W. Wilson Company, 1991), p. 51.

6. Newman, p. 38.

7. Ibid., p. 39.

8. *Outrageous!*, p. 128.

Chapter 5

1. Alan Richman, "Call Him 'Round Mound' at Your Peril; Charles Barkley's Bite is Worse Than His Woof," *People,* vol. 27, (April 27, 1987), p. 78.

2. Charles Barkley and Roy S. Johnson, *Outrageous!* (New York: Avon Books, 1992), p. 155.

3. Charles Barkley with Rick Reilly, *Sir Charles: The Wit and Wisdom of Charles Barkley,* (New York: Warner Books, 1994), p. 64.

4. *Outrageous!,* p. 274.

5. Ibid., pp. 284–285.

Chapter 6

1. Vern E. Smith and Aric Press, "Who You Calling Hero?," *Newsweek,* vol. 121, (May 24, 1993), p. 64.

2. Mel Reisner, "Barkley—Punch," Associated Press, (November 20, 1993), AP News. Online. Dialog.

3. Ibid.

4. Charles Barkley and Roy S. Johnson, *Outrageous!* (New York: Avon Books, 1992), p. 11.

5. Frank Deford, "Barkley's Last Shot," *Vanity Fair,* vol. 58, (February 1995), p. 124.

6. Ibid., p. 147.

7. Charles Barkley with Rick Reilly, *Sir Charles: The Wit and Wisdom of Charles Barkley,* (New York: Warner Books, 1994), p. xii.

8. Mark Jacobson, "The Trash-Talking, Butt-Kicking, Ball-Hogging, Love-Song Triumph of the Bad Chuck," *Esquire,* vol. 119, (May 1993), p. 136.

9. David Casstevens, *Somebody's Gotta Be Me: The*

Wide, Wide World of the One & Only Charles Barkley, (Kansas City, Mo.: Andrews & McMeel, 1994), p. 4.

Chapter 7

1. Mark Jacobson, "The Trash-Talking, Butt-Kicking, Ball-Hogging, Love-Song Triumph of the Bad Chuck," *Esquire,* vol. 119, (May 1993), p. 136.

2. Tom Knott, "Barkley's Golden Summer," *Washington Times,* July 24, 1992, p. M1.

3. Ibid.

4. Leigh Montville, "He's Everywhere," *Sports Illustrated,* vol. 78, (May 3, 1993), p. 85.

5. Bruce Newman, "A Double Feature All by Himself," *Sports Illustrated,* vol. 64, (March 24, 1986), p. 35.

6. Frank Deford, "Barkley's Last Shot," *Vanity Fair,* vol. 58, (February 1995), p. 124.

7. Charles Barkley and Roy S. Johnson, *Outrageous!* (New York: Avon Books, 1992), p. 221.

8. Charles Barkley with Rick Reilly, *Sir Charles: The Wit and Wisdom of Charles Barkley,* (New York: Warner Books, 1994), p. 64.

9. David Casstevens, *Somebody's Gotta Be Me: The Wide, Wide World of the One & Only Charles Barkley,* (Kansas City, Mo.: Andrews & McMeel, 1994), p. 142.

10. Barkley, *Wit,* p. 67.

11. Casstevens, p. 10.

12. Charles Moritz, *Current Biography Yearbook,* (New York: H. W. Wilson Company, 1991), p. 52.

13. Montville, p. 84.

14. Casstevens, p. 4.

15. Knott, p. M1.

16. Vern E. Smith and Aric Press, "Who You Calling Hero?," *Newsweek,* vol. 121, (May 24, 1993), p. 64.

17. "Ask Me Anything You Want!," *Sports Illustrated for Kids,* vol. 6, (May 1994), p. 52.

18. Barkley, *Outrageous!,* p. 325.

19. Tom Friend, "What You See Isn't What Barkley Is," *The New York Times,* May 30, 1993, sec. 8, p. 2.

Chapter 8

1. Greg Boeck, "Sir Charles' Capital Idea," *USA Today,* December 8, 1994, p. 3C.

2. David Casstevens, *Somebody's Gotta Be Me: The Wide, Wide World of the One & Only Charles Barkley,* (Kansas City, Mo.: Andrews & McMeel, 1994), p. 150.

3. Ibid.

4. Ibid., p. 156.

5. Michael Lutz, "Suns—Rockets," Associated Press (May 7, 1994), AP News. Online. Dialog.

6. Ibid.

7. Casstevens, p. 164.

8. Ibid., pp. 171–172.

9. Michael Lutz, "Optional," Associated Press, (May 21, 1994), AP News. Online. Dialog.

10. Ibid.

11. Boeck, p. 3C.

12. Mel Reisner, "Barkley's Return," Associated Press, (November 27, 1994), AP News. Online. Dialog.

13. *Official NBA Guide 1995–96,* (St. Louis: The Sporting News, 1995).

14. "Barkley Kids, but Who's Joke On?" *Washington Post,* (April 6, 1995), p. C13.

15. Ibid.

16. Knight-Ridder/Tribune Business News dispatch from Atlanta, (December 13, 1995). Online.

17. Paul Westphal, "Phoenix Suns," *Street & Smith's Pro Basketball*, (October 1995), p. 111.

18. Charles Barkley with Rick Reilly, *Sir Charles: The Wit and Wisdom of Charles Barkley*, (New York: Warner Books, 1994), p. 127.

19. Leigh Montville, "He's Everywhere," *Sports Illustrated*, vol. 78, (May 3, 1993), p. 88.

20. Ibid., p. 89.

21. Tom Knott, "Barkley's Golden Summer," *Washington Times*, July 24, 1992, p. M1.

22. Boeck, p. 3C.

23. Ibid.

24. "Ask Me Anything You Want!," *Sports Illustrated for Kids*, vol. 6, (May 1994), p. 53.

25. Samantha Stevenson, "Barkley: Ask Him a Question, He'll Tell You No Lies," *The New York Times*, January 9, 1994, Sec. 8, p. 9.

26. Ibid.

27. Alexander Wolff, "The Leaning Tower of Pizza," *Sports Illustrated*, vol. 60, (March 12, 1984), p. 60.

Career Statistics

COLLEGE

YEAR	TEAM	GP	FG%	REB	PTS	AVG
1981–82	Auburn	28	.595	275	356	12.7
1982–83	Auburn	28	.644	266	404	14.4
1983–84	Auburn	28	.638	265	423	15.1
Totals		84	.626	806	1,183	14.1

NBA

YEAR	TEAM	GP	FG%	REB	AST	STL	BLK	PTS	AVG
1984–85	Philadelphia	82	.545	703	155	95	80	1,148	14.0
1985–86	Philadelphia	80	.572	1,026	312	173	125	1,603	20.0
1986–87	Philadelphia	68	.594	994	331	119	104	1,564	23.0
1987–88	Philadelphia	80	.587	951	254	100	103	2,264	28.3
1988–89	Philadelphia	79	.579	986	325	126	67	2,037	25.8
1989–90	Philadelphia	79	.600	909	307	148	50	1,989	25.2
1990–91	Philadelphia	67	.570	680	284	110	33	1,849	27.6
1991–92	Philadelphia	75	.552	830	308	136	44	1,730	23.1
1992–93	Phoenix	76	.520	928	385	119	74	1,944	25.6
1993–94	Phoenix	65	.495	727	296	101	37	1,402	21.6
1994–95	Phoenix	68	.486	756	276	110	45	1,561	23.0
Totals		819	.555	9,490	3,233	1,337	762	19,091	23.3

Where to Write
Charles Barkley

Mr. Charles Barkley
c/o Phoenix Suns
P.O. Box 1369
Phoenix, AZ 85001

Index

A

Abernathy, Travis, 29
Ainge, Danny, 8
Alabama, University of, 31, 36
Atlantic City, New Jersey, 65
Auburn University, 29, 31, 32, 34–36, 38–39, 40, 75, 91

B

Barcelona, Spain, 72
Barkley, Charles
  birth, 21
  childhood, 21–26
  college career, 32–39
  in high school, 26–31
  marriage, 55
  NBA Draft, 41
  NBA MVP, 10
  Philadelphia 76ers, 41–49, 50–60, 61–65, 68–70,
  Phoenix Suns, 7–20, 70, 75–77, 80–87, 88–90
  Olympic Dream Team, 71–72
  wins scholarship, 31
Barkley, Christiana, 55–56, 68, 78–79
Barkley, Frank, 21, 24
Barkley, Maureen, 55, 63, 67, 72–73, 78–79, 83
Bird, Larry, 71

Birmingham, Alabama, 21, 30
Boston Celtics, 45, 47, 49
Breuer, Randy, 49
Bryant, Mark, 53

C

Catledge, Terry, 50
Charlotte Hornets, 53, 72
Cheeks, Maurice, 41
Chicago Bulls, 14–15, 17–18, 20, 58, 60
Cleveland Cavaliers, 50, 52, 58, 62
Coupland, Billy, 26, 29
Cunningham, Billy, 43, 44

D

Daugherty, Brad, 52
Dawkins, Johnny, 56, 58
Detroit Pistons, 49, 56
Dream Team, 71–72
Drexler, Clyde, 71
Dumars, Joe, 40–41

E

Edwards, Adolphus, 21–22
Edwards, Johnnie Mae, 21–22, 23, 24, 27, 63, 78
Erving, Julius, 41, 47, 50
Ewing, Patrick, 10, 14, 36, 71

F

Fitzsimmons, Cotton, 75
Foreman, George, 90

G

Garrison, Zina, 78
Georgetown University, 36
Glenn, Charcey, 21–24, 26, 27,
    34, 73, 75, 78
Glenn, Clee, 24
Glenn, Darryl, 24
Glenn, John, 24
Golden State Warriors, 81
Graf, Steffi, 78
Grant, Horace, 18
Green, Herbert, 29, 31, 32
Grosh, Dr. Julie, 54

H

Hawkins, Hersey, 63
Hinson, Roy, 50
Hollins, Lionel, 7
Hornacek, Jeff, 8, 70
Houston Rockets, 49, 82–83, 87
Hurt, Bobby Lee, 30–31, 36

I

Indiana Pacers, 53

J

Johnson, Kevin, 8, 10
Johnson, Magic, 10, 71
Jones, Bobby, 41
Jordan, Michael, 10, 14–15, 18,
    58, 71, 78
Joyner-Kersee, Jackie, 78

K

King, Martin Luther, Jr., 23
Knight, Bobby, 40–41

L

Laimbeer, Bill, 49, 56
Lang, Andrew, 8, 70

Leeds, Alabama, 21–25, 27,
    32, 36, 75
Leeds Elementary School,
    22–23
Leeds High School, 26–27,
    29–31, 34, 35
Leeds Junior High School, 26
Lister, Alton, 49
Los Angeles Clippers, 8
Los Angeles Lakers, 8, 12, 47
Louisiana State University, 36

M

Mahorn, Rick, 56, 58, 62
Majerle, Dan, 8
Malone, Moses, 41, 43, 45, 49,
    50, 52
Maxwell, Vernon, 83
Meadowlands, 66
Milwaukee, Wisconsin, 65–66,
    70
Milwaukee Bucks, 44–45, 49,
    52, 60
Minnesota Timberwolves, 8
Mokeski, Paul, 44–45, 49
Mutombo, Dikembe, 87

N

National Collegiate Athletic
    Association (NCAA),
    39
New Jersey Nets, 66
New York Knicks, 52
North Carolina, University
    of, 52

O

Olajuwon, Hakeem, 10,
    82–83, 87

Olympics
    1984, 40–41
    1992, 71–72
O'Neal, Shaquille, 10, 87
Orlando Magic, 87

P

Parrish, Robert, 72
Paxson, John, 18, 20
Perry, Tim, 8, 70
Philadelphia 76ers, 7–8, 41,
    43–45, 47, 49, 50,
    52–56, 58, 60, 61–63
Phoenix Suns, 7–8, 10, 12,
    14–15, 17–18, 70, 71,
    72, 75, 77–79, 80–84,
    87–88, 90
Pippen, Scottie, 18
Portland Trail Blazers, 10, 53,
    87
Puerto Rico, 90

R

Richmond Spiders, 39
Robinson, Cliff, 50

Robinson, David, 12, 87
Rodman, Dennis, 87
Rose, Lauren, 66–67
Ruland, Jeff, 50

S

San Antonio Spurs, 12, 84, 87
Seattle SuperSonics, 12, 14
Seles, Monica, 78
Silva, Jason, 68
Smith, Sonny, 32, 34–35, 39
Southeastern Conference,
    38–39

T

Thomas, Clarence, 91
Thomas, Isiah, 56
Tomjanovich, Rudy, 87
Toney, Andrew, 41, 50

W

Washington (Baltimore) Bul-
    lets, 44, 49, 50
Washington, D.C., 90
Westphal, Paul, 8, 88